THE NIGHT BEFORE CHRISTMAS

Clement Clarke Moore
and Anna Pomaska

DOVER PUBLICATIONS, INC.
Mineola, New York

NOTE

Delight in the beloved poem "The Night Before Christmas," by Clement Clarke Moore, as you color the charming illustrations by Anna Pomaska. On Christmas Eve, the cat family is visited by St. Nicholas and his reindeer, and Father spies St. Nick himself outside the bedroom window. The mouse asleep in its bed, the stockings hung by the chimney, and the bundle of toys—all will tempt you to color as you visualize scene after scene from Moore's verses.

Bibliographical Note

The Night Before Christmas is a new work, first published by Dover Publications, Inc., in 2000.

DOVER *Pictorial Archive* SERIES

International Standard Book Number: 0-486-41031-5

Manufactured in the United States of America
Dover Publications, Inc., 31 East 2nd Street, Mineola, N.Y. 11501

'Twas the night before Christmas,
when all through the house,

1

Not a creature was stirring, not even a mouse;

The stockings were hung by the chimney with care,
In hopes that St. Nicholas soon would be there;

The children were nestled all snug in their beds,

4

While visions of sugarplums danced in their heads;

And Mamma in her 'kerchief and I in my cap,
Had just settled our brains for a long winter's nap.

When out on the lawn there arose such a clatter,
I sprang from the bed to see what was the matter.

Away to the window I flew like a flash,
Tore open the shutters and threw up the sash.

8

The moon on the breast of the new-fallen snow,
Gave lustre of mid-day to objects below.

9

When, what to my wondering eyes should appear,
But a miniature sleigh, and eight tiny reindeer.

With a little old driver, so lively and quick,
I knew in a moment it must be St. Nick.

More rapid than eagles his coursers they came,
And he whistled, and shouted,
and called them by name;

"Now, *Dasher!* Now, *Dancer!* Now, *Prancer* and *Vixen!*
On, *Comet!* On, *Cupid!* On, *Donder* and *Blitzen!*

To the top of the porch! to the top of the wall!
Now dash away! dash away! dash away all!"

As dry leaves that before the wild hurricane fly,
When they meet with an obstacle, mount to the sky;
So up to the house-top the coursers they flew,
With the sleigh full of toys,
and St. Nicholas, too.

And then, in a twinkling, I heard on the roof
The prancing and pawing of each little hoof—

16

As I drew in my head, and was turning around,
Down the chimney St. Nicholas came with a bound!

He was dressed all in fur, from his head to his foot,
And his clothes were all tarnished
with ashes and soot.

A bundle of toys he had flung on his back,
And he looked like a peddler just opening his pack.

His eyes—how they twinkled!
His dimples—how merry!
His cheeks were like roses, his nose like a cherry!

His droll little mouth
was drawn up like a bow,
And the beard of his chin
was as white as the snow;
The stump of a pipe
he held tight in his teeth,
And the smoke it encircled
his head like a wreath;
He had a broad face
And a little round belly,
That shook when he laughed,
Like a bowlful of jelly.

He was chubby and plump, a right jolly old elf,
And I laughed when I saw him, in spite of myself,

A wink of his eye and a twist of his head,
Soon gave me to know I had nothing to dread;

He spoke not a word, but went straight to his work,
And fill'd all the stockings; then turned with a jerk,

And laying his finger aside of his nose,
And giving a nod, up the chimney he rose;

He sprang to his sleigh, to his team gave a whistle,

And away they all flew like the down of a thistle.

But I heard him exclaim, ere he drove out of sight,